Animal Tracks

by Sean Sanders
illustrated by Diane Blasius

Pre-Decodable 10

McGraw Hill Education

Bothell, WA • Chicago, IL • Columbus, OH • New York, NY

MHEonline.com

Send all inquiries to:
McGraw-Hill Education
8787 Orion Place
Columbus, OH 43240

ISBN: 978-0-02-138078-7
MHID: 0-02-138078-3

Printed in China

9 10 11 12 13 DSS 28 27 26 25 24

I see the .

snow

See the 

wolf

 ?

tracks

See the  deer  tracks ?

See the  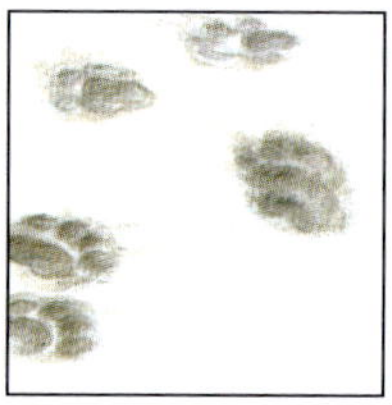 ?

rabbit tracks

See the  fox  tracks ?

I see the   !

animal tracks